LIFE CYCLE OF A
TREE

By Kirsty Holmes

LIFE
CYCLES

Words that look like **this** can be found in the glossary on page 24.

©2018
Book Life
King's Lynn
Norfolk PE30 4LS

Written by:
Kirsty Holmes

Edited by:
Holly Duhig

Designed by:
Daniel Scase

ISBN: 978-1-78637-286-4

A catalogue record for this book is available from the British Library.

PHOTO CREDITS

Photocredits:
Front Cover – kpboonjit, vovan. 1 – kpboonjit, vovan. 2 – Grisha Bruev. 3 – vovan, Alexey Laputi, amenic181, Dudarev Mikhail. 4 – Oksana Kuzmina, Melpomene, Pressmaster. 5 – Alliance, Elnur, Josep Curto. 6 – varuna. 7 – Elena Zajchikova. 8 – Gillian Dernie, LFRabanedo, Ross Gordon Henry, gostua. 9 – antoni halim. 10 & 11 – showcake. 12 – g-stockstudio. 13 – MagMac83. 14 – KevinTate. 15 – Ivan Galashchuk. 16 – Planner, Kittichai. 17 – Zerbor, Potapov Alexander. 18 – alekleks, Maryna_R, Aleksandr Bryliaev, rodho. 19 – Alex Tihonovs, axily. 20 – Don Mammoser. 21 – grad. 22 – amenic181, narikan. 23 – Fotofermer, Steve Photography, CHOATphotographer.
Images are courtesy of Shutterstock.com. With thanks to Getty Images, Thinkstock Photo and iStockphoto

LIFE CYCLE OF A
TREE

WHAT IS A LIFE CYCLE?

Baby

Toddler

Child

All living things have a life cycle. They are all born, they all grow bigger, and their bodies change.

When they are fully grown, they have **offspring** of their own. In the end, all living things die. This is the life cycle.

Teenager

Adult

Elderly Person

TREMENDOUS TREES

A tree is a type of plant. Trees have thick **trunks**, and branches covered in leaves. Trees also have roots which grow down into the ground and take in **nutrients** from the soil.

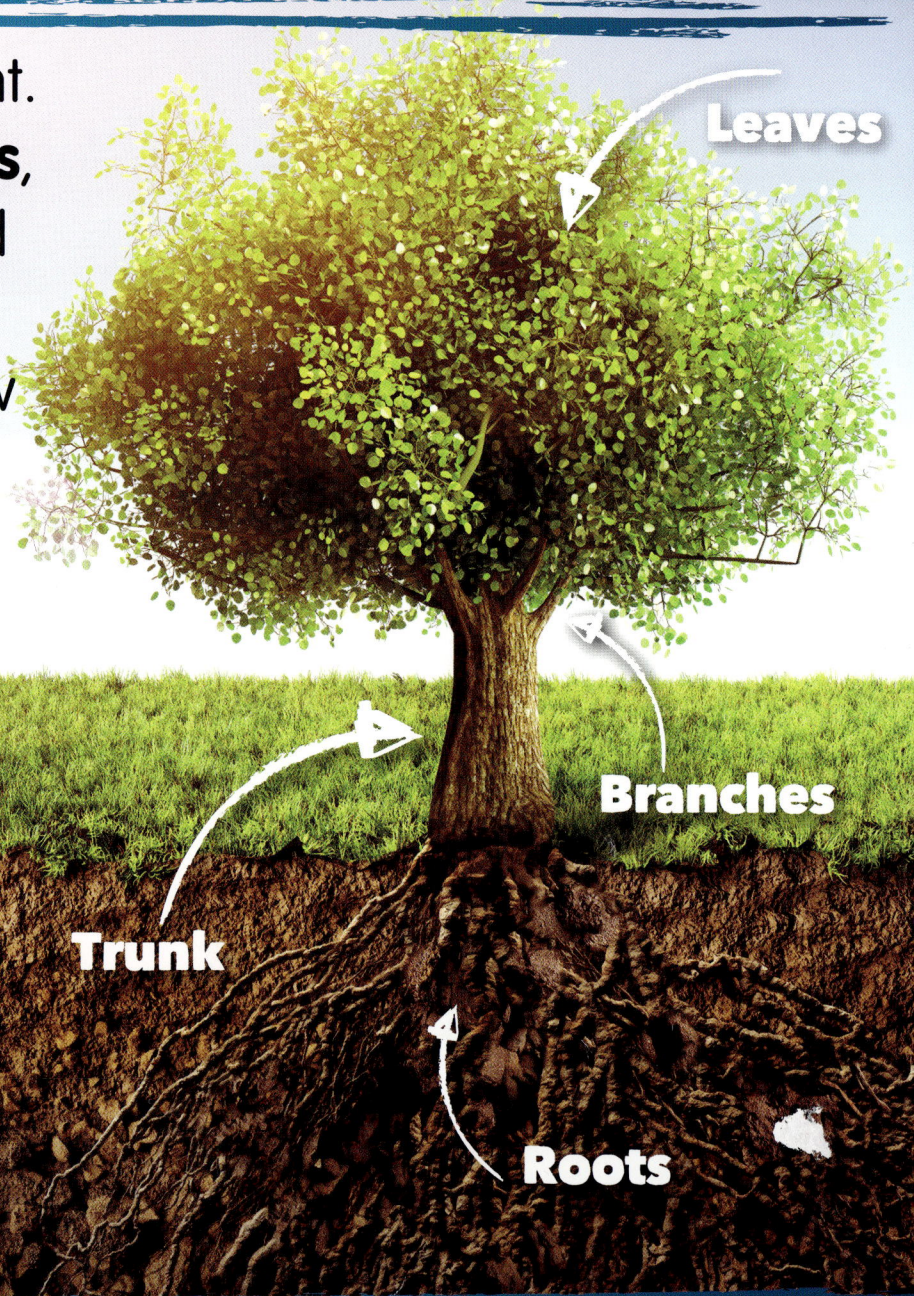

Leaves

Branches

A single tree can have many roots.

Trunk

Roots

Trees need water and **carbon dioxide** to live. They release **oxygen** which humans and animals need to breathe. Trees also need sunlight to make food.

SUPER SEEDS

Tree seeds are all different – some float on the wind, others are hidden inside nuts and fruit.

New trees are grown from seeds. Seeds need water to grow but they do not need food. They have their own food stored inside them.

Inside each seed, there is a tree **embryo** – a baby tree! The embryo has tiny leaves. Some trees spread their seeds on the wind. Some seeds are spread by animals and birds.

Cottonwood trees have fluffy seeds which fly on the wind.

SPRINGY SPROUTS

The seed **senses** if there is enough sunlight for it to grow. If there is, the seed takes water in from the ground until it bursts, and the embryo starts to grow.

This process is called 'germination'.

Radicle

Radicle Appearing

Seed

When this happens, a special root called a radicle will appear and grow down into the soil. Then the embryo will start to grow upwards forming a tiny tree. This is called a sprout.

Sprout

Why not try planting a tree of your own?

Leaves

SPECTACULAR SAPLINGS

As the sprout grows it forms a trunk which holds the tree up. It also grows deeper roots to hold the tree in the ground. At one metre tall, the sprout is called a sapling.

If we plant saplings, we must protect them from danger.

Saplings are still small, and their trunks are quite soft. They can freeze, run out of water, be trampled on or eaten by wildlife.

TERRIFIC TREES

Trees grow tall so their leaves can reach enough sunlight to make food.

Fully grown trees are called mature trees. They will usually grow very tall, and spread out lots of roots and branches.

Once a tree is mature, it will make its own seeds.
These will look the same as the seed that made the tree!

Apple Tree

LIFE AS A TREE

All trees need water, sunlight, and nutrients from the soil to make food and keep growing. Trees need the right sort of weather, too.

Some trees like cold weather, and some like hot, **tropical** weather.

Evergreen trees are trees with leaves that stay green all-year-round. Deciduous trees have leaves that turn brown, golden or red in the autumn, and fall off.

FUN FACTS ABOUT TREES

- Tree trunks have rings. If you count the rings, you can tell how old a tree is.

- **There are more than 60,000 different types of tree.**

- Bonsai trees are special Japanese trees that are grown to be tiny.

• The manchineel tree in Florida is the most poisonous tree in the world. A single bite of its fruit can kill a person!

DO NOT
EAT!

• **Some trees can live for thousands of years. A Great Basin bristlecone pine in the USA is known to be over 5,000 years old!**

• The world's tallest tree is called Hyperion, a coast redwood in California. It is over 115 metres tall!

• Antarctica is the only continent in the world with no trees.

Most trees will never die of old age. As long as they have the right **conditions** they will keep on growing. Trees die because of **drought**, flooding or diseases, or because they are eaten or chopped down.

A tree that has died but still stands is called a 'snag'. Sometimes, the snag will **rot** and break down, returning its nutrients to the ground, ready for new life to grow.

THE LIFE CYCLE

Trees have a complete life cycle. This means their life cycle has separate stages. All the stages are different.

Seed

Sprout

Sapling

Mature Tree

Snag

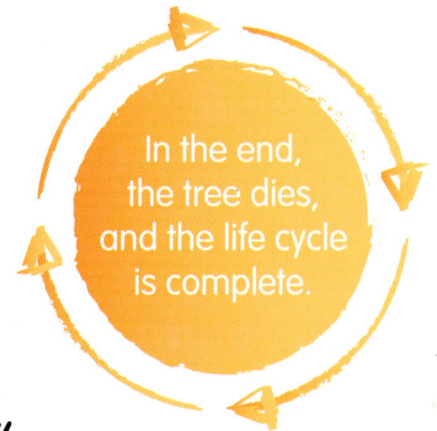

In the end, the tree dies, and the life cycle is complete.

The seed germinates and becomes a sprout. The sprout grows, forms a trunk, and becomes a mature tree. The mature tree produces seeds of its own.

23

GLOSSARY

carbon dioxide	a natural, colourless gas that is found in the air
conditions	the state of the environment needed for something to happen
drought	a long period of very little rainfall, which leads to a lack of water
embryo	an unborn or unhatched young in the process of development
nutrients	natural substances that plants and animals need to grow and stay healthy
offspring	the child or young of a living thing
oxygen	a natural gas that all living things need in order to survive
rot	break down or decay
senses	discovers or notices something
tropical	hot and humid
trunk	the thick, woody stem of a tree

INDEX